PAST TIES

AND

COLOURED EYES

HILLARYANNE

HILLARYANNE

ISBN: 978-1-9995157-0-6

DEDICATION

To those who inspired it
and may never read it,

and to letting go.

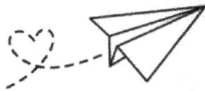

CONTENTS

ACKNOWLEDGMENTS

It is no understatement that every inch of my heart
has been written into this book

May you fall completely in love, every time you open
it

Thank you for reading, I am forever grateful

xx

LACUNA EYES
Lacuna: a blank space, a missing part.

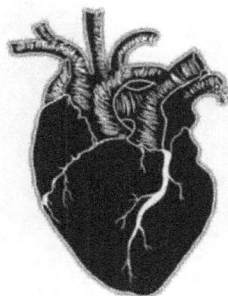

HILLARYANNE

Although you occupied
a large piece of my heart
you always felt
like a missing part
a blank space
the truth, I
avoided to face

He was different
than anyone I've ever known
maybe that's why
he spent all his time alone

That night, the moon was blue
that night, I couldn't help falling
for you
that night,
oh how I wish I could undo

You lit a fire
so bright in my soul
I cannot put it out
and although I love
the warmth of it,
it's burning me alive

You held the gun to my heart
and I pulled it closer
daring you to hurt me
remaining my composure
you pulled the trigger

I loved the rollercoaster

I remember you
with a wave of regret
loving what we had
and wishing
we never met

You played the strings
of your guitar
so beautifully
I thought you'd do the same
with the strings of my heart

HILLARYANNE

I miss the danger in your eyes
I miss that love, your demise
the torture of your words
the dark in the skies
that darkness won't leave,
no matter how hard I try

Be honest
this fragile heart
can't take another lie,
tell me straight
although I'm afraid, this heart
may die

Oh God,
what I'd give
to feel again

And it's not till I think about you
that I become someone else

I saw your face
through the busy street lights
and in my chest, I felt a fire
ignite

I've searched all these years for revenge
and only found myself
wanting more

I'm left with scars
all over the place
no matter what I do
your memory
I can't erase

Your song plays in my head all day long
but I'll never be able to hit pause
I'm not that strong

I can try and leave
go somewhere new
but the stars and the moon
will never forget
what I did to you

Your love was temporary
and I knew that,
but I pretended like it wasn't
like when you think the ink is dry
but still smudges

It was your demons
that made me leave
not you.

c,

You gave me the gift of music
tied in a bow
it once was yours
but you decided to let it go
you passed it onto me, in hopes
my talents would grow
but how can my fingers
make it flow
when you were the only
type of music, I used to know

The less of you I need
the more I get

I ask myself
when will these feelings subside
I can't help but feel
a piece of my heart has died

I change with the seasons
was my excuse
for leaving

Although I love the sea
I've never been a fan
of salty eyes
and that's all you gave me

I tried to kill
what was killing me
and by accident, I
killed your memory

I was in love with you,
I promise, I was
I felt like nothing else
could measure up,
no such thing as a stronger love
I promise, I was in love with you
until he,
walked in the room

HILLARYANNE

OCEAN EYES

HILLARYANNE

I can't help but miss your smell
miss my smell with you
miss the smell of midnight cigarettes
clinging
to my long tangled hair,
the smell of the air

HILLARYANNE

I watched myself
break your heart
like a car crash,
so sudden
I couldn't look away
I'm sorry I abandoned you
but what was there left
for me to say

It's frightening knowing
how dark
the deepest parts of you can be
like discovering
the depths of the sea

Georgia,

both a place,
and a person

He said, show me your scars
so I rolled up my sleeves, and
he stopped and said
no
the ones on your heart

I've always wanted to learn piano,
to be proud of my fingertips
for doing something
other
than missing the feeling
of your midnight skin

It all started with
your lips in the winter;
the warmth of your breath
and the heavy whisper

HILLARYANNE

Why I do this to myself, I'll
never know
something comes over me
and I can't let you go

I do not trust
where my 3am mind goes
when I am alone
in my dark lonely room
doing nothing
but missing you

It was those midnight cigarettes
with the moon and stars
where I'd confess to you
all my scars

With fear
I'm longing
to tell him
he's all
I'm needing

HILLARYANNE

Out of all the ways
the world could tempt me
your lips
by far
outweigh them all

Here I am
adding tar to my lungs
ignoring the enviable, pretending
I'll always
remain young

2am,
3pm,
5am
it's all the same
the thought of you
lingers in my brain
I swear, I
could go insane

A reckless night
accompanied by the city light
on the highest hill in your town
is enough to make me turn this car
around

HILLARYANNE

I untie my hair
and lay my body in bed
regretting all those things
I never said

My heart is in the east
but it belongs in the north, with you
I've never been good at direction
so as I touch my finger tips
to this old wrinkled map
I imagine a life where finding
how to get to you, came easily

I was leaving

the last time I'd walk out your door
and the first time I'd never come back
and all I remember feeling
were your lips
begging me to stay

Would you meet me
in between the bliss
of the raging ocean waves
and the calm night sky
would you meet me in between
the mistakes of him, and I
could you meet me, where I lost myself
that day in June, when I left your house

HILLARYANNE

I'm sorry I couldn't see this through
but thank you for the view
my ocean eyes
my raw blue

And then came the tide
and my love for you
died

HILLARYANNE

MIDNIGHT EYES

HILLARYANNE

I had never known
what it was like
to swim in the sea
until I met you
and you made an ocean
in me

May you always be
my expectations
and not
my reality

You're my favorite kiss
my favorite place to miss
my favorite tear to cry
by your side
I hope
I die

HILLARYANNE

Stay near to those
who feel like the morning sun
on your tired toes

I want to see
the northern lights
reflected off your eyes
I want to see
vast mountains
competing with your shoulders
I want to see
the midnight stars
jealous of you
for shining brighter
I want to see
the whole world
with just you
and me

HILLARYANNE

Where to baby?
I have a toothbrush in my bag
and a soul
desperate for adventure

You are beautifully
and solely a work of art
stitched together piece by piece
and made with a fragile heart

Your worth to me
is more important
than my morning coffee

Feel my breath
like tender wind against your chest
feel my pulse
pounding like thunder through these walls
feel my love
like endless rainfall from above
I am a storm
hoping you notice me, transform

HILLARYANNE

I am quite short
and have never wished to be tall
for tall people see too much at once
and can't enjoy the view
of what it looks like
to be looking up
at you

I wonder what you think
when you see my curled hair
my hazel eyes and my pink lips
can you see my broken heart
do I wear it on my sleeve
or does it hide, wishing to be seen

Love is a feeling
I've never been able to explain
like the sun being out
when it starts to rain

One look
is all it took

HILLARYANNE

"Put your heart into mine", he said
so I took my heart out
and put it back in, as if
for the first time

The groves of his collarbone
told me stories
so beautifully written

HILLARYANNE

I could fall completely apart
if you'd ever dare
to break my heart

Eyes as dark as the midnight sky
soul as soothing as a lullaby
lips that make me endlessly fly
how could I ever say
goodbye

HILLARYANNE

It was that feeling
at 5:29pm
when your cold sheets touched
my naked thigh
that I knew
this feeling would never die

Life isn't always what it seems
but I swear your just as perfect
as my dreams

Leave me
in your warm sheets
in the cold of morning
cover my toes before you leave
brush back my hair
from crowding my face
and before you go,
take my heart with you, for it
was always yours
in the first place

My problem is
I expect too much
of you
I expect you to look at me
the way
I can't help but
look at you

HILLARYANNE

Tell me with the absence of fear
that you can't live this life
without me near
without that, I'm afraid it's not enough
for me to stay here

Some pair wine with food
but I pair the night
with you

HILLARYANNE

I collect books
like scars on my skin
none from you, and
all from him

I'm finding every excuse I can
to see the darkness in you
but I'm afraid I cant
for you are pure love, through
and through

HILLARYANNE

I'm hoping this is right
because times running fast
and it'll kill me
if this doesn't last

Tell me sweetheart, because I can't decide
is this love worth fighting for
or has it already died

HILLARYANNE

Your body I'll forever abide by
I simply touch your skin
and my nerves amplify

Oh how naïve
to think I could live without you

HILLARYANNE

THROUGH HER EYES

HILLARYANNE

There's no chance
that in 50 years
I'd look back on this life
and wish I would've loved more
because I have loved
everything
and everyone
with every inch of my soul
and that
I am most proud of

She had an unordinary
and unmeasurable
love for the moon
as if she'd meet it some day

stupid dreamer

Don't deprive yourself
of feeling emotions
even if they hurt
you'll grow so much more
knowing how it feels
to have your heart in
p i e c e s

I realized something

that little things in this life
inspire me
like the way the rain settles on a leaf
or the calm I feel
at a red light after midnight
I realized this life has more to offer me
than part time jobs
and loads of homework
and that these words deserve
to be written into a book
that airplanes
are the closest thing we have
to truly being near to the moon
that there are no goodbyes
but only
'I'll see you soon'

Sad

people

tell

beautiful

stories

HILLARYANNE

Sometimes

the more simple the words are
the more they break your heart

I pulled over to admire
the stars in the sky
they make me feel less alone, they
make me feel
alive

The only thing beautiful
about the dead,
is when the leaves change
from green to red

I'm still running
from all the mistakes
hoping soon
these chains will break

HILLARYANNE

Life isn't a race
although people make it out to be
take your time
take water breaks
take time to stretch
hell,
finish last if you want
as long as you make it to the finish line
nothing else matters

I think it's quite a beautiful art
the way people can illustrate
a broken heart

HILLARYANNE

I looked out to the view in front of me
and couldn't believe
I had waited and lived
all this time
without ever really knowing
the beauty this world holds

My greatest strength
and my biggest weakness
is that I am in fact
a dreamer
and will never wish
to be anything else

HILLARYANNE

How do you stop yourself?
from falling completely in love with
your memories
and completely out of touch
with reality

They say its vampires and werewolves
that wake with the fullness of the moon
but what about the dreamers,
the broken hearted,
and the hopeless romantics
that come out too

HILLARYANNE

Since when was it a bad thing
to think like a child,
for our minds are polluted
and theirs are so beautiful
and wild

The earth gives more to those
who appreciate
the grass and the soil
dirtying their toes

HILLARYANNE

And what scares me the most
is
there is so much of me
left untouched

PAST TIES AND COLOURED EYES

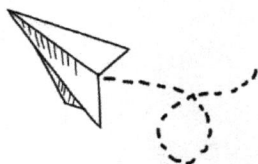

HILLARYANNE

ABOUT THE AUTHOR

Hillary-anne is a 22 year old girl with dreams as high as the stars. She was born in Ontario, Canada in the dead of winter, with a heart on fire. For a young girl, she has been through many trials and life experiences that have given her the inspiration to put it all into poetry. She is a dreamer, an adventurer, a nurse, a writer, an artist, a lover, a fighter and a lifelong learner. Through this journey of becoming a new self-published author and poet, she has learned that you can always chase your dreams, no matter how crazy they might be. Always trust in yourself and don't let anyone or anything, get in the way of what your heart is telling you to do.